GREAT MOMENTS IN

THE WORLD SERIES

GREAT MOMENTS IN

THE

WORLD

SERIES

EDWARD F. DOLAN, JR.

FRANKLIN WATTS
New York / London / Toronto / Sydney / 1982
A TRIUMPH BOOK

Photographs courtesy of: National Baseball Hall of
Fame and Museum: pp. 2, 7; United Press Inter-
national: pp. 12, 23, 35, 42, 52, 54, 61, 64, 76;
Pittsburgh Pirates: pp. 39, 44; New York Mets:
pp. 50; Philadelphia Phillies: pp. 70, 74, 75

Library of Congress Cataloging in Publication Data

Dolan, Edward F., 1924–
Great moments in the world series.

(A Triumph book)
Includes index.
Summary: A brief history of the World Series,
focusing on outstanding games and players.
Includes a list of participants since 1903.
1. World series (Baseball)—History—
Juvenile literature. [1. World series (Baseball)
2. Baseball—History] I. Title.
GV863.AID64   796.357′782′09   81–19809
ISBN 0–531–04409–2   AACR2

R.L. 2.7 Spache Revised Formula

CONTENTS

GREAT MOMENTS IN

THE WORLD SERIES

CHAPTER ONE
1884
A GREAT IDEA

"He's really something to see."

That's what baseball fans were always saying about James Mutrie. He was a big man with a thick, curly mustache. He liked stovepipe hats, the kind President Lincoln used to wear. Mutrie wore them all the time, even when he was in uniform.

"And he's a top manager."

That was something else the fans were always saying. They had a good reason for saying so. In 1884, Mutrie was managing the New York Metropolitans. His team had been winning all season long.

There were two professional baseball leagues at the time, the American Association (AA) and the National League (NL). The Metropolitans played in the American Association. The way things looked, Mutrie and his Mets were sure to win the AA pennant.

"He's also a man with a great idea."

The man "with the great idea"—
James Mutrie of the New York Metropolitans.
He's seen here without his stovepipe hat.

What great idea were the fans talking about? Mutrie saw that the rival National League also seemed to have a sure pennant winner. These were the Providence Grays up in Rhode Island. Mutrie had an inspiration.

"The Mets and the Grays should play a championship game," he told himself. "The two pennant winners going at each other. It would be terrific! It would show who's got the best team in the country."

Mutrie fired off a telegram to the Grays:

I INVITE YOU TO NEW YORK . . .
TO PLAY A CHAMPIONSHIP GAME
WITH THE METROPOLITANS . . .
DO YOU ACCEPT THIS CHALLENGE?

The answer came within a few days. It surprised Mutrie. The Grays didn't think much of his idea. They weren't a bit interested in coming to New York.

"All right," Mutrie thought, "maybe they want to play in front of their own fans."

So off went another telegram. This time, Mutrie challenged the Grays to *two* games. One would be played in Rhode Island, the other in New York City. The teams would split the money they took in at the gate.

Again, the Grays had just one thing to say: "No, thank you."

Providence didn't explain why it refused to play. But Mutrie was sure he knew the reason. He told the newspapers that he thought the Grays were afraid.

His comments reached Providence. Now it was Mutrie's turn to receive a telegram—an angry one. It said the Grays would come to New York. They would play a series of games against the Mets. Each team was to put up $1,000. The winner would take all the money. Agreed?

Mutrie grinned and jammed his stovepipe hat down on his head. "You bet it's agreed."

The teams decided to play a three-game series. Glaring at each other, the opposing players met for the first time on Thursday, October 23, 1884. It was all the wrong weather for baseball. The skies were gray. A cold wind was blowing. About 2,500 fans came. They sat in wooden grandstands and shivered.

Just before game-time, the two captains walked to the plate. A coin was tossed in the air. The Grays captain won the toss. He chose to have the Mets bat first. The day was yet to come when the visiting team would always be first up.

The crowd settled back to watch the game.

They knew it would be a good one. But they had no idea that it was going to be something more. It was going to be a historic one.

Why?

Because many people say that one of today's greatest sports events began that afternoon in 1884. They say that the Mutrie series marked the start of the World Series. In the years to come, millions of Americans would think of nothing but baseball for a few magic days each October.

Actually, Mutrie's series was not the first one ever tried. Cincinnati won the American Association pennant in 1882. That team challenged Chicago of the National League to a championship series. It was called off after a couple of games because of an argument between the two leagues. The AA and NL had thought about another series in 1883. They never got together for it.

But the 1884 series would be played all the way through. Also, the NL and AA had stopped fighting by now. They gave the series their approval. It became an official championship battle. So, many people think of the game on October 23 as the first in the World Series. They say that the day was full of historic firsts.

Charles "Old Hoss" Radbourn of the Grays was the first man to pitch a ball in World Series history. He had a terrific record for the year. Providence was short of hurlers, and so Hoss had started 73 games. He'd never been taken out of a game, not once. One day, he would find a place in baseball's Hall of Fame.

The Mets' shortstop, Jack Nelson, was the first man at bat in Series play. He also was the first man to post an out.

Providence outfielder Paul Hines came to bat. Tim Keefe was on the mound for the Mets. A pitch got away from him. The ball smacked Hines in the ribs. Hines became the first Series player to reach base for being hit with a pitch.

Keefe worked well. He and Radbourn kept the score at 0–0 until the seventh inning. Then Keefe put a pitch right where second-baseman Jack Farrell wanted it. There was a sound like a gunshot. Farrell took off. He watched the ball sizzle into deep center. It hit the ground and bounced high. Farrell rounded first. Then he was standing at second, with the first double in Series history.

Moments later, shortstop Art Irwin slammed a triple off Keefe—another first. Farrell raced home. He scored the first Series run. Irwin posted the first RBI.

Keefe was a top pitcher. He had 35 wins on the season. In a few years, he would win 19 games in a

Tim Keefe, the Metropolitans'
ace pitcher. The Grays slugged him
off the mound in game 3.
But he stayed and helped
to fill in as umpire.

row. Like Radbourn, he was headed for the Hall of Fame. But today the Grays got to him. They walked off with a 6–0 win.

It was another Series first, a shutout. But the fans had missed the best first of all. They hadn't seen a home run.

They saw one the next day. Third sacker Jerry Denny came to bat for the Grays in the fifth. There were two runners on base. Denny put all his muscle into his swing. The ball sailed high, then dropped into the bleachers.

How many fans saw that homer? Just 1,000. The weather was so bad that most fans stayed home. Indeed, it was so cold that the game was called after seven innings. The Grays were leading 3–1 at the time. They had their second win.

The weather was even worse for game 3. Only 300 fans showed up. They watched the Grays drive Keefe right off the mound.

Then they saw a real baseball oddity. When Keefe left the mound, he didn't head for the locker room. He stayed and filled in as umpire. The fans said he did an honest game.

He must have. When the game was called because of darkness, the Grays were beating his Mets 12–2.

The series was over. Calling themselves "the champions of the United States," the Grays went home in triumph. The Mets were given a parade. More than 300 amateur ball clubs came to New York to march in the parade. James Mutrie was driven through town in a stagecoach.

The AA and NL decided to play a series each year. They began calling it the World Championship Series in 1886. In 1903, it was officially named the World Series.

Between 1886 and 1900, nine games were usually played in each Series. One year the leagues got very ambitious. They put on a 15-game affair. The teams traveled to ten different cities, leaving the players exhausted. The 4-out-of-7 Series that we know today began in 1905. There were exceptions in 1919, 1920, and 1921 when 5-out-of-9 Series were played.

The American Association folded in 1890. The National League teams played the Series among themselves for a few years. Then the American League (AL) was formed. The AL and NL began their Series battles in 1903. What is called the modern World Series dates from that year.

The autumn battles continue to this day. They have given us one great moment after another.

Let's look now at some of the greatest of those moments.

CHAPTER TWO
1929
THE BIGGEST RALLY

How about these great moments for a start?

1905

NEW YORK GIANTS (NL)

vs.

PHILADELPHIA ATHLETICS (AL)

Christy Mathewson ranks as one of the finest pitchers in the history of the Giants. He pitched three games against the Athletics. The right-hander threw a shutout every time. It was a record that has never been equaled in Series play. The Giants won the Series 4 games to 1.

1929

CHICAGO CUBS (NL)

vs.

PHILADELPHIA ATHLETICS (AL)

A manager once made his players grin when he said: "It ain't good to be behind when the game's over."

The fact is, it's not good to be behind anytime. And it's disastrous to be down by eight runs in hot Series action.

That's where the Philadelphia A's were in the bottom of the seventh in game 4. But they went on to make history. They staged the wildest rally in Series play.

The A's had easily taken the first two games from Chicago. But the Cubs came battling back to win game 3. Now they were threatening to run away with game 4. It was being played at Philadelphia. Chicago first baseman Charlie Grimm nailed a two-run homer in the fourth. A batch of singles added five runs in the sixth. Another in the top of the seventh brought a man in. Chicago held a whopping 8–0 lead.

By now, the Philadelphia fans were disgusted. For them, the game was as good as over. They began heading for the exits. They didn't know it, but the fun was about to begin.

A's outfielder Al Simmons opened the bottom of the seventh. He was a power hitter. And he proved it. He drove the ball high and deep. It finally thumped down on the roof of the left field stands.

*Al Simmons is greeted at the plate
after nailing a homer. The ball landed
on the roof of the left field stands.
With Al's shot, the Philadelphia A's
began the wildest rally in Series history.*

Simmons circled the bases in triumph. But all he got from the crowd was some tired applause. Al knew how the fans felt. Sure, they liked the homer. But they knew that it did little good.

"Well," he told himself, "at least we won't be shut out."

It was going to be anything but a shutout. The A's now clubbed four singles in a row. Two of the hitters came home on them. The other two hitters were on base and ready to score. The gap had narrowed to 8–3.

Outfielder Bing Miller had rapped out one of those singles. He sailed the ball to center. He was certain that the Cubs' fielder, Hack Wilson, would gather it in. But the sun blinded Wilson. The ball hit the ground. Bing was safe at first.

The four hits got the crowd stirring. Look at that! 8–3! There were two men on and no outs . . .

Then the whole stadium groaned. A pinch hitter came up for the A's pitcher. He popped up. One away.

A moment later, the crowd was roaring. Second baseman Max Bishop stepped into the box and connected. The ball headed straight for the mound. But it was high and sizzled above the pitcher's outstretched glove. It landed behind second and skidded into shallow center. One of the base runners charged home.

8–4! Philadelphia was halfway to a tie! And there were still two men on base!

It was time for the Cubs to switch pitchers. Starter Charlie Root, who had pitched great ball until now, was sent to the showers. In came southpaw Art Nehf. Nehf would be on the mound for the biggest play in the game, if not in the entire Series.

It all started when he fired the ball to the next batter, outfielder Mule Haas. A power hitter, Haas lashed a shot to deep center. Fielder Hack Wilson moved back for the catch. It promised to be easy. Wilson looked up for the ball . . . .

And, as before, the sun hit him full in the eyes. Blinded, Wilson faltered. Then he stumbled. He tried to shade his eyes with his glove. It didn't help. He couldn't see a thing. He heard the ball thud behind him. It bounded to the barrier. Wilson spun and started looking for the ball.

Haas reached first. He made the turn and gunned for second. He could see the two runners ahead of him streaking home. Then he was past second and sprinting to third. The coach was signaling wildly. Keep going! That meant just one thing. Wilson hadn't gotten the ball yet. OK! Haas touched the bag. Driving hard, he started for home.

But finally Wilson had the ball. He fired it to the infield. It was relayed from second to the catcher. Haas saw the throw coming. With a final burst of speed, he charged safely across the plate.

Three runs were in. The A's had closed the gap to 8–7. And Haas had earned himself something rare—an inside-the-park home run.

There was no holding the Philadelphia fans back now. They were on their feet and roaring. They roared when their catcher, Mickey Cochrane, strode to the plate. They roared when he got a walk. They roared when Nehf was pulled out of the game. And they roared when Sheriff Blake came in to replace him.

Blake lasted for just two hitters. Right off, Al Simmons came up for his second go in the inning. He sent a grounder to his left. The ball bounced hard and sailed high over the third baseman's head. Simmons pulled up at first. Cochrane went to second.

The next batter, Jimmie Foxx, pounded a single through the hole to center. Simmons raced to second. He saw Mickey Cochrane going all the way home. Simmons had never heard so much noise in his life. The stadium sounded as if it were jammed to the rafters.

8–8!

Even the A's themselves couldn't believe what was happening. They'd tied things up. They still had two runners on base. And there was still only one out. They had a real chance to push ahead and win.

Pat Malone replaced Blake on the mound. Everyone in the park knew that Malone could give Philadelphia trouble. He was the ace of the Cubs' staff. The fans watched Bing Miller walk to the plate for the second time in the inning.

Miller's first pitch sailed too far inside. The ball clipped Miller. He whirled out of the box. There were gasps in the stands, followed by sighs of relief. Miller wasn't hurt. He trotted to first. The two runners ahead of him advanced a base, with Simmons going to third. It was the hard way for Bing to get on base. But he didn't mind. He could think of just one thing: the sacks are loaded.

And the crowd was thinking of just one thing when Jimmy Dykes came up. Wouldn't it be great if the third sacker could hit a homer—a grand slam? Then we'd have seen *everything* in this crazy inning.

Jimmy was thinking grand slam, too. He put all his muscle into his swing. Crack! Jumping up and screaming, the fans watched the ball rocket into deep left. It seemed sure to fall into the stands. But

• 16 •

it landed right at the wall. It was quickly scooped up. Back it shot to the infield.

The runners were almost a blur on the base paths. Simmons came home from third. Foxx scored behind him. Bing Miller went from first to third. And a grinning Jimmy Dykes braked at second. He'd missed his grand slam by just inches But he was the proud owner of a double.

The score now stood 10–8, with the A's out front.

The fans were breathless and hoarse. But who cared? They were watching a miracle. Actually, at that moment, the miracle was over.

Pitching hard, Malone struck out the next batter. He then repeated the performance with a pinch hitter.

The wildest rally in Series history had come to an end.

The A's held their lead and walked off with game 4. Then they nailed down game 5 by a 3–2 margin to become the 1929 world champions. But they had to explode with another rally to get the job done.

Going into the ninth, they were trailing 2–0. Mule Haas tied things up with a two-run homer over the right field wall. Moments later, Bing

Miller doubled almost to the scoreboard. Al Simmons scored from second with the winning run.

It was a fine rally, but not as great as the one the day before. Nothing could be as great as *that* one.

CHAPTER THREE
1932

THE BABE
CALLS HIS SHOT

More great moments:

1930
ST. LOUIS CARDINALS (NL)
vs.
PHILADELPHIA ATHLETICS (AL)

The Series was tied at two games apiece. Game 5, the tie breaker, went scoreless until the ninth inning. Then Philadelphia's powerful first baseman, Jimmie Foxx, came to bat. He belted a two-run homer. That's all it took. The A's won, 2–0, and went on to take the Series, 4–2.

1932
CHICAGO CUBS (NL)
vs.
NEW YORK YANKEES (AL)

Babe Ruth walked to the plate.

It was the top of the fifth in game 3. Ruth's Yankees were playing at Chicago. They were locked in a 4–4 tie with the Cubs. The scoreboard showed one out. The bases were empty. Ruth was the second man to bat in the inning.

He was also the greatest slugger of his time. The Babe had started as a pitcher with Boston. Then he'd moved to the Yankees. They switched him to the outfield because of his batting ability. As an outfielder, he could bat every day. He walloped 60 homers in the 1927 season. It was a record that remains unbroken.

But, that day, the Babe wasn't being treated like a baseball great. The Chicago crowd roared with anger as he walked to the plate. Some lemons sailed out of the stands. There were taunting shouts from the Chicago dugout. Ruth heard someone yell, "You big ape!" It was one of the nicer names that came his way.

This Series had turned into one of the hottest ever played. These two teams were great rivals. The Yankees had whipped the Cubs in games 1 and 2 at New York. They'd slugged them dizzy, winning 12–6 and 5–2.

Now the Yanks had come to Wrigley Field for game 3. They were in the heart of enemy territory.

Everyone was letting Ruth know it.

Charlie Root stood on the mound. He stared in at the plate. He went into his windup. The ball slammed into catcher Gabby Hartnett's mitt.

Strike 1!

The crowd loved it. There was laughter and applause—and more insults for the Babe from the Cubs dugout. Ruth knew pitcher Guy Bush was leading the jeers. He felt a rush of anger.

Ruth stepped out of the box. His eyes flashed and he turned to the dugout. He saw Bush standing there. The two men glared at each other.

Then Ruth angrily shook his bat at the dugout. His lips moved. With his free hand, he pointed out toward the diamond.

A gasp ran through the crowd. Ruth seemed to be doing just one thing. He was telling the Cubs where he planned to hit the ball: to center for a home run. The nerve of the guy!

"He's good," someone said. "But not *that* good. *No one's* good enough to call his shots like that."

Ruth set himself for the next pitch. Again, Charlie Root let the ball fly. It crossed the plate.

Strike 2!

There were more cheers from the stands. The insults from the Chicago dugout were worse than ever. Two strikes! The great Bambino was about to strike out. He was about to be shamed in front of 50,000 people. He'd learn. He'd never call another shot, never again.

But look!

Again, Ruth plunged out of the box. Again, he glared at Bush and the Cubs. Again, he shook the bat. Again, he pointed toward center.

The fans stared in disbelief. "Get that guy! He's almost out and he still won't quit."

"He's making a fool of himself."

The crowd waited for the next pitch. Charlie Root decided on a change-up. The ball arrived high and inside. Ruth swung hard. Crack!

Suddenly, the stands were a sea of movement. People jumped to their feet. They craned their necks to follow the ball. It headed for deep center and sailed high. Center fielder Johnny Moore raced back for it.

But Moore knew he was wasting his time. He pulled to a stop. The ball cleared the bleacher screen in deep center. It landed at the base of the stadium flagpole. Homer!

Stunned, the crowd watched the Babe trot around the bases. He might be a hated Yankee. But everyone had to admit one thing. The greatest hitter of his time had kept his promise. He'd homered *and* he'd homered to center. He'd really called his shot.

*Homer! Babe Ruth sends the ball
out of the park in the 1932 Series.
Ruth's "called shot" in game 3
became a baseball legend.*

It was one of the greatest moments in Series history. New York went on to win the game, 7–5. The Yankees then slugged their way to the world championship the next day. But the fans could only think of Babe's homer. It would become a baseball legend that would never die.

Babe Ruth's "called shot" is more than a great sports yarn. It's also a mystery story.

Sports reporters wrote that everyone had seen Ruth point to center. But no one had heard him say he was going to send a homer there. Everyone had simply guessed that he planned to do so.

Well, maybe everyone had guessed wrong.

It was risky to promise a home run—and to an exact spot—in front of 50,000 people. So maybe the Babe had been doing something else when he shook the bat and pointed. Then he got lucky and ended up looking like a superman.

But what could that "something else" have been? Ruth himself would never say. He loved publicity. So he just sat back and let the mystery grow.

Charlie Root said that he could solve things. He claimed that Ruth didn't point to center. Rather, the Babe held up his hand to signal the number of strikes.

Yankee slugger Lou Gehrig wouldn't buy that.

Gehrig had been in the on-deck circle while Ruth was batting. Ruth, he said, had definitely pointed to center. He'd meant to send the ball there, no doubt about it.

Then a story went around that Ruth had visited a hospital before the game. He stopped at a sick child's bedside and promised to hit a homer for the youngster.

Finally, years later, Charlie Grimm spoke up. The Cubs star had his own version of the "called shot." It was an interesting one. He put it into his book *Baseball, I Love You,* which was published in the 1960s.

Grimm had been Chicago's player-manager on that day long ago. According to Grimm, the Cubs went into the game really angry. They'd taken a bad beating in games 1 and 2. And besides, there was the hassle over shortstop Mark Koenig.

Mark had been with the Yankees for several years. Then he had played for the Detroit Tigers. He'd come to the Cubs last August. He helped them win the NL pennant by hitting a solid .353. Afterwards, the Chicago players got together and decided on how to split their coming World Series pay. They voted to give Koenig just a small cut. After all, he had been with the team for such a short time.

The vote angered the Yankees. Their former

teammate deserved better treatment, they said. They accused the Cubs of being cheap. The entire city of Chicago was furious at the insult. Wrigley Field seethed with anger on the day of game 3.

Then Babe Ruth capped things off. Just before game-time, he walked over the Chicago dugout. He sighted Koenig and called to him. No one knows exactly what the Babe said. But his words went something like this: "Hey, Mark! Who are those cheapskates you're sitting with?"

After that, the Cubs wouldn't let Ruth alone. They insulted him whenever he came to the plate. The insults were particularly bad in the fifth. Leading the name-calling was pitcher Guy Bush. He was due on the mound next day for game 4.

Charlie Grimm saw Ruth step out of the box after strike 1. He saw him glare at Bush. He saw him shake the bat. He saw him point.

But, Charlie explained, the Babe *hadn't* been shaking the bat at the entire dugout. He'd been shaking it at Bush. And Ruth *hadn't* been pointing to center field. He'd been pointing out to the *mound.*

And, Charlie said, Ruth had yelled to Bush: "Wait till you're out there tomorrow. Then we'll see what you can do against me."

And so the Babe hadn't been calling his shot at

all. He'd been warning Bush. He delivered the same warning again after strike 2. At least, that's what Charlie Grimm said.

Then Ruth homered and gave the World Series an undying legend.

Some people believed Charlie Grimm's story. Some didn't. To this day, the mystery has never really been solved.

Did the Babe call his shot or didn't he? Who knows? And who really wants to know? The story is perfect just the way it is.

CHAPTER FOUR
1956

PERFECT GAME

Still more great moments:

1940
CINCINNATI REDS (NL)
vs.
DETROIT TIGERS (AL)

Bobo Newsom pitched game 1 for the Tigers. He was really proud of his 7–2 win. His dad had come up from South Carolina and was in the stands. But early the next day, terrible news reached Bobo. His father had died of a heart attack during the night.

Though grief stricken, Newsom pitched game 5. It was a dandy—an 8–0 shutout. Bobo said that he pitched it for his dad.

But it was for a losing cause. Cincinnati took the Series from Detroit, 4–3.

1956

BROOKLYN DODGERS (NL)
vs.
NEW YORK YANKEES (AL)

"OK," Don Larsen told himself, "let's go."

The tall right-hander took his set for the pitch. He made himself forget the roar of the crowd. He looked at the plate. He saw batter Junior Gilliam digging in. He let the pitch fly . . . .

Game 5 of the autumn battle with the Dodgers began with that throw. The ball sailed in off-target. Gilliam watched it go by. Plate umpire Babe Pinelli shouted: "Ball!"

It wasn't much of an opening pitch. It didn't show Larsen that he was in for a fine day, a day he would never forget.

There were 64,519 people in Yankee Stadium that October 8. They had no idea how sharp Larsen was going to be. In fact, the Yankee fans were worried. They felt their team might be in trouble with Larsen on the mound.

Sure, they said, he's a good pitcher. A hard thrower with an odd delivery. He throws without a windup. It drives some batters crazy.

But—

There was his record for the season. It hadn't

been too hot—11–5. And, his control could be a problem. His pitches often went haywire.

The fans were remembering what had happened in game 2. Larsen had been the starting pitcher. The Yanks had given him a beautiful 6–0 lead in the second. But then the Dodgers got to him. They filled the bases. Larsen was sent to the showers. Brooklyn went on to a 13–8 victory.

Now the Series was tied at two games each. Larsen was back on the mound. The Yankee fans were sweating. Would the hated Bums get to him again?

They didn't. The first inning went perfectly. After his opening pitch, Larsen fanned Gilliam. Next, shortstop Pee Wee Reese went down on a called strike. Then outfielder Duke Snider lined to right for the final out. The Yankee fans grinned at each other.

There was a bad moment, though, in the second. Third baseman Jackie Robinson fired a shot between second and third base. But the Yankee shortstop charged in fast. He scooped up the ball and threw it across the diamond. Jackie was out at first by less than a step.

After that, things calmed down. The third inning passed quietly. So far, Larsen had faced nine batters. He'd retired them all. Four had gone down on strikes. The Yankee fans went on grinning at each other.

But they were still worried about Larsen. His teammates hadn't given him any runs. He needed a lead. Every pitcher did.

Center fielder Mickey Mantle took care of the problem in the fourth. He sent a drive toward the right field stands. The ball headed straight for the foul pole. It missed the pole by inches on the inside and dropped into the stands. Mantle trotted around the bases to make the score 1–0.

Larsen started the fifth by getting Jackie Robinson to fly to right. Then came a really bad moment. First sacker Gil Hodges stepped up and swung hard. The ball flew into deep left-center. It seemed about to drop in. But Mickey Mantle raced over. Out went his glove as far as it could reach. The ball smacked into the webbing.

The sixth inning rolled by. The Yankees added another run. Then came the seventh. One by one, the Dodger batters went down. Larsen now had six strikeouts. A hush began to fall over the stadium. One thought was forming in everyone's mind.

There were no hits or runs for Brooklyn. There were no errors for anyone. Larsen was working on something very special, something even better than a no-hitter . . . .

Some fans didn't want to say what that "something" was. They believed in an old baseball superstition. Talking about the "something" would ruin the pitcher's chances.

But they couldn't stop from thinking about it: "Don's got a perfect game going."

It seemed an impossible goal. Bill Bevens of the Yankees had come close to a no-hitter in the 1947 Series, only to lose it in the ninth. But no one had ever really gotten near a perfect game in Series play. And there had been few perfect ones in regular season action. There had been only six since organized ball began in the 1870s.

Up in the press box, a reporter turned to a friend. "Bet you don't know who pitched the last one."

"You'd win."

"Charlie Robertson of the Chicago White Sox. Back in 1922."

The friend whistled. 1922. That was 34 long seasons ago.

Both men shook their heads. It was too tough a goal to reach, especially in the pressure cooker of World Series play. Larsen would never make it. Something was bound to go wrong.

They were almost right. Jackie Robinson came to bat in the eighth. He slashed the ball right back to the mound. Larsen reacted with lightning speed. He grabbed the ball, whirled, and threw to first—in time.

Then it was the ninth. Every eye in Yankee Stadium followed Larsen to the mound. The pressure on him had to be awful. He knew he was three outs away from the impossible. If only he could hold together . . . .

Catcher Yogi Berra crouched behind the plate. Carl Furillo stepped into the box. The outfielder was a dangerous man, very dangerous. There was no windup from Larsen, as usual. The ball sailed in. A foul. Strike 1.

The second pitch. Another foul. Strike 2.

Next, a high one for a ball.

A fan groaned. "Don't *do* that, Don. Get him! Get him!"

Now two more fouls. Then there was a sharp crack of the bat. The fans sprang to their feet. The ball sailed high. It came down in right field. Hank Bauer stood under it for the catch.

One away!

Brooklyn's fine catcher, Roy Campanella, walked to the plate. After hitting a foul, he connected. The ball bounded to second base. Billy Martin snared it for the throw to first—and the out.

Two down! Just one more to go.

Suddenly, a worried rumble went through the stands. Pitcher Sal Maglie was due up next. As expected, the Dodgers were sending in a pinch hitter. But he was veteran Dale Mitchell. This was bad. Mitchell was sharp with the bat.

Larsen had now thrown 92 pitches in the game. He stared in at Mitchell and fired pitch 93—for a ball outside. Umpire Babe Pinelli called the 94th a strike. Mitchell swung hard at 95 . . . and missed.

Just one more strike to go. That's all Larsen needed.

But Mitchell nailed pitch 96. Again, the fans jumped up. The ball shot into the left field stands for a foul. Yankee Stadium sighed with relief.

Still just one more strike to go.

Mitchell dug in, his bat flicking. Larsen took his set. The ball came sailing in. Mitchell thought it was outside. He started to swing, checked himself, and let it go by, only to hear Pinelli shout: "Strike!"

It was over! Pitch 97 had done the job. Mitchell turned to argue with Pinelli. But his words were lost in the thundering roar from the stands. Yogi Berra went dancing out to the mound. He jumped high and landed in Larsen's arms. Then both men were gone from sight, hidden in a mass of wild Yankees.

The scoreboard says it all!

*Yankee Don Larsen delivers one of the final
pitches in his perfect outing against the
Dodgers. He pitched the only perfect game
in Series history—so far, that is.*

The Yanks had seen perfection. They were letting Larsen know it.

Larsen threw 97 pitches that afternoon. He recorded 7 strikeouts, 13 flies, 5 infield grounders, and 2 line drives to the infield. His was not only the first perfect game in Series history. It was also an achievement that, to this day, has never been equaled.

The 2–0 victory gave the Yankees a 3–2 edge in the Series. The Dodgers evened things up in game 6 by winning 1–0. Then in game 7, the New York bats came alive. Berra homered twice. Outfielder Elston Howard followed with a homer of his own. And first baseman Bill Skowron wrapped things up with a grand slam. The Yankees won the game, 9–0.

The "perfect game" Series was over. New York had another championship flag.

CHAPTER FIVE
1960

THE
BOUNCE-BACK PIRATES

Some fantastic Series action
occurred in the 1950s.

1957
MILWAUKEE BRAVES (NL)
vs.
NEW YORK YANKEES (AL)

Right-hander Lew Burdette of the Braves came
close to tying an old record this year. Remember
those three shutouts that Christy Mathewson
threw back in 1905? Well, Burdette hurled three
wins against the Yankees. Two of them were shutouts. Milwaukee took the Series 4–3.

1960
PITTSBURGH PIRATES (NL)
vs.
NEW YORK YANKEES (AL)

The 1960s opened with one of the most exciting championship battles ever seen. This was the Series of the "bounce-back" Pirates.

Happy. This was the only word for the Pittsburgh Pirates. After failing many times, they had finally made it back to the Series. They hadn't been there since 1927.

The Bucs were matched against a very powerful Yankee team. The Yankee crew went on to break all kinds of Series records. They scored 55 runs and rapped out 91 hits—the most ever posted. They sported a team batting average of .338. It was the highest ever for a seven-game Series.

Their second baseman, Bobby Richardson, set some records of his own. He batted in 12 runs for the Series, six of them in one game. Both feats were Series highs.

As powerful as they were, the New Yorkers should have had an easy time. But they didn't.

Here's what happened in game 1. Right off, Yankee outfielder Roger Maris hit a homer. But then the Pirates came to bat, and the bounce-back started.

The first man up, outfielder Bill Virdon, got a walk. He headed for second on the next pitch—a strike to shortstop Dick Groat. Behind the plate, Yogi Berra jumped up. He fired the ball to second.

*Bill Virdon. He's now one of the
most respected managers in baseball.*

But no one was covering the bag. Virdon raced safely to third.

Then he dashed home when Groat doubled. Next, Groat crossed the plate on a single by outfielder Bob Skinner. Finally, the great Roberto Clemente hit the ball to center. Skinner came in to score.

The inning closed with the Pirates leading, 3–1. They went on to win, 6–4.

There was no bounce-back, though, in game 2. The Yankees were red-hot at the plate. They got 19 hits. Two were homers by Mickey Mantle. Mantle drove the first into the right field stands. The second sailed 475 feet (145 m), over the center field wall.

The final score could have belonged to a football game: 16–3, New York.

Nor was there any bounce-back in game 3. This time, the Yanks rapped out 16 hits. Bobby Richardson tagged a grand slam in the first inning. He later brought in two runs with a single. He had his Series high of six RBIs in a single game. It was quite a day for a man who had batted just .252 in the regular season. The grand slam was only his second home run for the year.

Again, the score could have belonged to a football game: 10–0. But things changed in game 4. It was bounce-back time again.

As usual, the Yankees took the lead first. They jumped ahead 1–0 on a homer. But in the fifth inning, Pittsburgh pitcher Vernon Law sent a double to the fence in left. A runner shot home. Moments later, Bill Virdon singled with two men on. Both runners scored. The Pirates moved out front, 3–1.

New York closed the gap to 3–2 in the seventh. Then, late in the inning, Yankee batter Bob Cerv almost tied things up. He drove the ball 400 feet (122 m) into right center. It dropped right at the fence. But Bill Virdon was there. He jumped high and slammed against the fence—and came down with the ball in his glove.

That was it for the day's scoring. The game ended 3–2 in favor of the Bucs.

The Series was now tied, 2–2. The Pirates continued their winning ways in game 5. They held the hot Yankee bats to just five hits and took a 5–2 win.

Then it was time for the Yankees to bounce back. They came through in game 6. They nailed 17 hits for a 12–0 win. Bobby Richardson had another field day at the plate. He got two triples.

Again the Series was even, this time 3–3. The championship would be decided in game 7.

By game-time, 36,683 people were in the stands at Pittsburgh. They were thinking of the terrible

beating that the Pirates had just taken. They wondered if the Bucs could bounce back for a last time. It didn't seem possible.

But right from the start, the Pirates looked tough. First baseman Rocky Nelson homered into the stands in the first inning. Two runs scored. In the second, two men raced home on a single by Bill Virdon.

Pittsburgh held a 4–0 lead until the fifth. Then the Yankees started to cause trouble. Bill Skowron homered to make things 4–1. Bobby Richardson opened the sixth with a single. He came home on a shot to center by Mantle.

Then, with two men on, Yogi Berra lumbered up to the plate. He slammed the ball safely into the upper deck in right. The Yanks were now inches ahead, 5–4. They moved out to a 7–4 lead with two runs in the top of the eighth.

But then there was a Pirate bounce-back in the bottom of the inning. Dick Groat singled a run home. Roberto Clemente did the same. And catcher Hal Smith sent the ball over the left field wall for a three-run homer.

Bill Virdon grabs a hit by Bob Cerv.
Number 21 is Roberto Clemente.

*Bill Mazeroski ended the 1960 Series
with a game-winning homer for
the Pirates. A top second baseman,
he's seen here in double play
action during the season.*

The Pirates were in front again, 9–7.

But not for long. Mantle singled in the top of the ninth. Berra grounded to first. Both brought in a run. Things were now even at 9–9.

The game went into the bottom of the ninth.

To the Pirate fans, it didn't look good. Second baseman Bill Mazeroski was due up first. Though a good hitter, he hadn't been too sharp that day. Yes, he'd bunted safely. But then he'd popped to short and grounded to second.

Mazeroski stepped into the batter's box. Facing him out on the mound was reliever Ralph Terry. Terry delivered his first pitch. Mazeroski let it go by. It was too low to suit him. The second one arrived a little higher. "Maz" liked it. He swung . . . and watched the ball streak out to left.

And then he watched it disappear over the scoreboard!

The game was over, 10–9. So was the Series, 4–3. The Pirates had the 1960 championship.

Mazeroski trotted around the bases. When he reached third, the base path was lined with shouting and dancing fans. They knew that New York had come to the Series with the greatest bats in baseball. But the Pirates had come with something even better. They'd come with the ability to bounce back.

CHAPTER SIX
1969

THOSE
MIRACLE METS

Record-breaking pitching . . . A miracle . . .
These were the highlights of the 1960s.

1968
ST. LOUIS CARDINALS (NL)
vs.
DETROIT TIGERS (AL)

Bob Gibson of the Cardinals outdid himself in
game 1. The right-hander fanned 17 Detroit
Tigers. He set a new record for the most strikeouts
in one Series game.

Gibson started three games. In them, he sent 35
batters back to the dugout. Gibson became the top
strikeout artist in Series history. The old record,
set in 1964, had been 31 strikeouts for an entire
Series.

Who held the old record? If you guessed Bob
Gibson, you guessed right.

Despite his fine work, the Tigers managed to grab the championship, 4–3.

1969
NEW YORK METS (NL)
vs.
BALTIMORE ORIOLES (AL)

It was a year of miracles.

Astronaut Neil Armstrong became the first man to walk on the moon.

And, the New York Mets made it to the World Series. Many fans joked that it was the bigger of the two miracles.

The Mets had been formed in 1962 when the National League was expanded. Their full name was the New York Metropolitans, the same as James Mutrie's team in 1884. But Mutrie's men had been pennant winners. The modern Mets weren't.

The New Yorkers spent their first years losing game after game. Their helpless brand of ball endeared them to countless fans everywhere. There are always people who love to root for the underdog.

Then, in 1969, the Mets suddenly got it all together under manager Gil Hodges. In August, they started to win—and didn't stop. From nine and a half games back, the New Yorkers surged to the front of their division. They closed the season eight games ahead of everyone else. The Eastern Division crown was theirs. The newspapers called them "those Amazin' Mets."

1969 was a historic year for baseball. Both the AL and the NL had been expanded to 12 teams each. Each league had been split into two divisions —the Eastern and Western Divisions. For the first time, the teams that won their division pennants went against each other in a playoff series for their league pennant. The play-off winners then headed for the World Series.

In the NL play-offs, the Mets beat the highly favored Atlanta Braves in three straight games. Gil Hodges and his club had the NL pennant. They were in the Series. Now the papers were calling them "the *Miracle* Mets."

But most fans didn't expect another miracle. The Mets had done the impossible in coming this far. Now they had to face the Baltimore Orioles, a real powerhouse club. The Orioles had taken their division title by 19 games. And they had swept the Minnesota Twins in the AL play-offs.

No, the fans said. The Mets would never be able to beat Baltimore. No way!

It looked like the fans were right in game 1. The

first Oriole up was outfielder Don Buford. He took one pitch from Tom Seaver. The ball whistled over the right field fence. Baltimore went on to a fairly easy 4–1 win.

"That's it," everyone thought. "The miracle's over."

But the Mets had other ideas. They now gave the baseball world some moments it would never forget. For instance, who could ever forget the Mets' pitching in game 2?

Starter Jerry Koosman held the Orioles hitless for six full innings. They finally managed two singles in the seventh. But Jerry kept putting the ball where Baltimore couldn't find it. Then, leading 2–1 in the ninth, he gave up a couple of walks. Ron Taylor came on to relieve. He tied down the win by getting third baseman Brooks Robinson to ground out.

Next, who could forget center fielder Tommie Agee's catches in game 3?

New York was ahead 3–0 in the fourth. But the Orioles were threatening. With two outs, they had two men on base. Catcher Ellie Hendricks rifled the ball to deep left-center. Tommie Agee came racing across for it. He made the catch right at the wall, backhanded. The side was out. And the score was still 3–0.

Then, in the seventh, Baltimore threatened

*Southpaw Jerry Koosman. He kept
putting the ball where the Orioles
couldn't find it in game 2.*

again. As before, there were two outs. But this time the bases were loaded. Paul Blair nailed the ball to right-center. Again, Agee came charging across. The ball seemed beyond his reach. Tommie hit the ground and skidded on his stomach for 10 long feet (3 m). But the ball was in his mitt.

Tommie's catches stopped Baltimore from taking a big lead. The Mets headed for the showers with a 5–0 win. The fans went home shaking their heads. It was impossible! The Mets—the *Miracle* Mets—were leading the Series, 2–1.

And next, who could ever forget the crazy ending to game 4?

The game, tied 1–1, was in the tenth inning. Catcher Jerry Grote started things for the Mets with a double. Rod Gaspar went in to run for him while second baseman Al Weis came to the plate. The Orioles gave Weis an intentional walk so that they could get to pitcher Tom Seaver. But the Mets sent in pinch hitter J. C. Martin instead.

Martin bunted in an effort to move Gaspar to third. Relief pitcher Pete Richert grabbed the ball and threw to first. But the throw went wide of the bag. The ball hit Martin on the wrist and bounded away. Gaspar streaked around third and came home with the winning run.

The Orioles protested the play. They argued

that Martin had run illegally into foul territory at the time the ball hit him. They also claimed that he had interfered with Richert's throw. But the argument did no good. The umpires wouldn't reverse their decision. (Photos later showed that the Orioles were right.) The Mets—who'd believe it?—had stretched their Series lead to 3–1.

And, finally, who could ever forget "the shoe polish adventure" in game 5?

It happened in the sixth inning. Trailing 3–0, the Mets were up. Outfielder Cleon Jones was at bat. A pitch sailed in too low. There was a stirring of dust at Cleon's feet. He jumped back in pain. Then he started toward first. But he heard the plate umpire call him back.

The umpire signaled for him to go on batting. Jones said that the ball had nipped his left foot. The umpire shook his head. The ball had hit the ground. But it had not touched Cleon's foot.

Crash dive! Tommie Agee makes his spectacular catch in the seventh inning of game 3. With the bases loaded, Paul Blair of the Orioles drove the ball to right center. Tommie skidded on his stomach for 10 feet (3 m). He came up with the ball.

*Cleon Jones looks on during the
"shoe polish adventure" in game 5.
Manager Gil Hodges shows umpire
Lou DiMuro a smudge on the ball.
It proved Jones had been hit
on the foot by a pitch.*

Out of the dugout came manager Gil Hodges. He argued that the batter had been hit. The umpire went on shaking his head. At last, the men at the plate called for the ball. They looked it over and Hodges grinned. He had all the proof he needed. The ball was smudged with shoe polish. A happy Jones headed for first.

Moments later, first baseman Donn Clendenon homered to left. Cleon loped home. He waited at the plate to shake Clendenon's hand. They had closed the gap to 3–2.

Al Weis homered to tie things up in the next inning. Then came the eighth. Cleon doubled. He crossed the plate on another double, this one by outfielder Ron Swoboda. Then Swoboda scored when two Orioles mishandled a grounder by Jerry Grote.

And that was it. The Mets held the lead for the rest of the game. They ended up with a 5–3 victory and the world championship for 1969.

New York City went wild. There were parades and celebrations everywhere. The National League fans in the city had hated to lose their Giants and Dodgers to the West Coast. But now they could forget those losses. Now they had new champions—the best champions of all.

They had the Miracle Mets.

CHAPTER SEVEN
1977

HOME RUN
KING

The 1970s were not to be outdone by the 1960s. There was lots of great action throughout the decade. And the October battle gained a new home run king.

1972
CINCINNATI REDS (NL)
vs.
OAKLAND A's (AL)

Oakland catcher Gene Tenace was the hero of this Series. He put together an amazing Series record. Gene led the players on both squads in homers, runs batted in, runs scored, and total bases. He batted .348 and had a slugging average of .913. In the first five games, he cranked out four home runs.

It was quite a performance, especially for a man who had been the team's second-string catcher. Tenace had hit only .225 in the regular season.

The "Swingin' A's" took the championship from Cincinnati, 4–3.

1977
LOS ANGELES DODGERS (NL)
vs.
NEW YORK YANKEES (AL)

Gene Tenace joined some fine company when he hit those four homers. The Yankees' Babe Ruth, Lou Gehrig, and Hank Bauer had each done it once. Duke Snider of the Dodgers did it twice. Each had also posted four round-trippers over the course of a Series. No one had been able to do better.

In addition, Babe Ruth had held a batting record of his own. He had been the only player ever to hit three home runs in a single Series game. In fact, he'd done it twice. He got the first three in game 4 of the 1926 Series. The next three came in 1928, again in game 4.

Four homers in a Series, three in a single game. They were both great records. But now it was 1977. And a man in a Yankee uniform was going to do something about them.

He was outfielder Reggie Jackson.

Everyone knew that Jackson was one of the greatest sluggers around. He'd proved it during his long career with the Oakland A's. And he'd proved it this year in his first season with the Yanks. His 32 homers had helped bring New York to the Series battle with the Dodgers.

But everyone was worried about Jackson as play began. He seemed to be having trouble with the bat.

Game 1 was played at Yankee Stadium. In the first inning, Jackson hit the underside of the ball. It flew high and dropped into shallow center, a bloop single, nothing to get excited about.

But this turned out to be Reggie's best shot of the day. He popped up in the fourth. He got on base in the sixth—thanks to being hit by a pitch. Then in the eighth, there was another walk for him. And that was it. The game ended 4–3 in favor of the Yankees.

Things were no better for Jackson in game 2. In fact, they were worse. Reggie went down on a called strike in the second. Next, he grounded into a double play. Then he was fanned. Finally, he drove the ball high—right to the center fielder.

The Dodgers won the game, 6–1. The Series was tied at one game each.

Game 3 was in Los Angeles. Things now looked better for Reggie. He came to bat in the first and sent a low drive to left. The Dodger fielder played the ball on the hop. He bobbled the grab. Jackson didn't even pause at first. He dashed for second and pulled up safe. Then he went the rest of the way home on a single by outfielder Lou Piniella.

Reggie had hit the ball well. But he wasn't out of trouble yet. He was fanned twice, in the third and in the seventh. In between, he got on base with a walk. It was all he could do that day.

The game ended in a 5–3 victory for the Yankees.

Even though their team was leading in the Series, the New York fans wanted more action. Would Jackson ever really connect? Reggie answered them in game 4.

In the second inning, his hard, smooth swing sent the ball screaming high above third base. It stayed just inside the foul line. Jackson watched it travel almost to the left field wall. He went into second with a solid double.

But Reggie didn't do so well in the third. He flied to left. Finally, in the sixth, he gave the New York fans what they had been waiting for. He swung hard, so hard that he almost went down on one knee. But he connected—solidly. The ball took off like a rocket. It sailed into the left field pavilion.

At last! A homer!

A smiling Reggie Jackson trotted around the bases. After that, he ended his day with a fly to left-center in the ninth. The Yankees had their third win in the Series—a 4–2 victory.

The New York fans were hoping for another homer in game 5. At first, they were disappointed. Jackson flied out on his first two trips to the plate. Next, he hit a single.

But then in the eighth, a pitch came in right over the plate. Reggie pounded the ball to deep right. For a moment, the whole stadium held its breath. The ball was heading straight for the foul pole. It hit the pole. Then it shot into the stands in fair territory.

Another Jackson homer! This was more like it!

But the homer was in a losing cause. The Dodgers got 13 hits that day. They took the game 10–4. They closed the gap to 3 games to 2.

By now, the New York fans weren't so disappointed in Jackson. At least, he'd nailed two homers in two days. He seemed to be coming out of his slump. The fans now wanted to see what he would do in game 6 at Yankee Stadium.

Reggie Jackson starts to swing.
He connected for his second homer in
the 1977 Series against the Dodgers.
This homer came in the eighth inning.

They didn't know it, but he was about to make baseball history.

It started in the fourth inning. There was one Yankee on base. The Dodgers were leading, 3–2. Jackson came up to face starter Burt Hooton. Earlier, the right-hander had given him a walk.

Hooton delivered his first pitch. The ball arrived right where Jackson wanted it. He swung hard and smoothly. There was a sharp crack. The ball turned into a white comet. It went hurtling toward the right field stands.

Jackson watched the ball as he ran to first. He saw it disappear into the stands. Then he circled the bases while the crowd roared. It was a two-run homer and Jackson's third round-tripper of the Series. The score was now 4–3 in favor of the Yankees.

It was all that any New York fan could ask for.

But there was more to come. Jackson returned to the plate in the fifth. The Yankees had added another run, making the score 5–3. Starter Hooton was now gone for the day. Reliever Elias Sosa stood out on the mound. There was one man on base.

Sosa let the ball fly. Then history repeated itself. The pitch came in where Jackson wanted it. He swung hard and smoothly. There was that sharp crack. The ball went hurtling into right and disappeared into the stands!

The roar in Yankee Stadium sounded like thunder. The fans were on their feet. They'd just seen back-to-back homers, each worth two runs. The Yanks now had a 7—3 lead.

And Jackson now had four homers in the Series. Those fans who really knew their baseball history were impressed. "Hey! Wait a minute. Four homers. He's just tied the Series record."

They were right. Jackson had become the sixth man ever to belt out four homers in a Series. He'd joined Babe Ruth, Lou Gehrig, Hank Bauer, Duke Snider, and Gene Tenace.

Jackson would come to bat again in this game. What if he could get another homer? He'd set a new record—five round-trippers. And he'd do something else. He'd have three homers in a single game. He'd tie Babe Ruth's record.

Three homers back-to-back. It seemed too much to expect, even for a slugger like Reggie Jackson.

Jackson's next turn at bat came in the eighth. The bases were now empty. There was a new pitcher on the mound—knuckleballer Charlie Hough. Elias Sosa had headed for the showers after the homer in the fifth. He was followed by Doug Rau who had pitched for a few innings.

The crowd held its breath as Hough went into his windup. Could Jackson possibly do it? The ball came sailing in. . . .

Jackson swung. Again, there was that crack and the roar of the crowd. Again, the ball became a white comet. But it didn't head to right this time. It started for center. And it kept going and going —until it landed in the bleachers.

Once again, the fans were on their feet as Jackson circled the bases. There was the thunder of a standing ovation for the new record: three back-to-back homers, five homers for the Series, and three for a single game.

The World Series had a new hero.

That third homer was the last big hit of the day. The Yankees had an 8–4 win. The 1977 championship was theirs, 4–2.

Reggie Jackson's three homers were unusual. Not only were they hit back-to-back. But each was also hit on the first pitch. And each was hit off a different Dodger hurler.

It was quite a feat—even for baseball's new home run king.

There she goes! Reggie Jackson
watches one of his shots take off.

CHAPTER EIGHT
1980

DOUBLE
TROUBLE

1978
LOS ANGELES DODGERS (NL)
vs.
NEW YORK YANKEES (AL)

Game 3 belonged to Yankee third baseman Graig Nettles. He turned in four great defensive plays. These kept the Dodgers from winning and from taking a powerful lead in the Series.

It was the third inning. Dodger outfielder Reggie Smith grounded a bullet to the side of third base. Graig lunged for the ball and caught it backhanded. He threw Smith out at first.

Then it was the fifth inning. The Dodgers had one out and two men on base. Again, Smith fired a shot to third. This time, the ball screamed above Graig's head. He jumped high and knocked it down. This kept a run from scoring, and Smith was held to a single.

But the bases were loaded. First baseman Steve Garvey drove the ball hard at Nettles. Graig snagged it for an out. He threw to second for a force-out. The side was retired.

The Dodgers loaded the bases again in the sixth. There were two outs when infielder Dave Lopes connected. The ball sizzled along the ground wide of third. Nettles moved with lightning speed. The ball disappeared into his glove. Then it went flying to second for another force-out. The Dodger threat was over.

Helped by Graig's fine plays, the Yankees posted a 5–1 victory. They won the championship, 4–2.

1980
PHILADELPHIA PHILLIES (NL)
vs.
KANSAS CITY ROYALS (AL)

It was the eighth inning of game 6. A moment ago, the fans in Philadelphia's Veterans Stadium had been wildly happy. Their Phillies held a 4–0 lead. The team was just six outs away from winning the 1980 Series. But now the fans were worried.

The Royals had a real threat going. Until now, they hadn't scored once off the Phillies' great left-hander, Steve Carlton. But he was tiring. He'd opened the eighth by walking catcher John Wathan. Then outfielder Jose Cardenal had gotten on base with a single.

But the worried fans grew hopeful when manager Dallas Green came out of the dugout. Carlton left the game to a standing ovation from the crowd. In came his replacement—the stocky Tug McGraw, Philadelphia's ace reliever.

Tug had relieved in games 1, 3, and 5. He'd done a great job every time. The fans were sure that he could handle the Royals. A win would tie the Series down.

This would be great. The Phillies had been around since 1883. For years, they had shared the town with the Philadelphia A's of the American League. The A's had won five championships before moving away. But the Phillies had been in only two Series, in 1915 and 1950. They'd lost them both. Now the long wait for the Series flag seemed just about over. If only Tug could come through.

McGraw looked sharp on his first pitches. He got second baseman Frank White to foul out. But oh no! The fans were worried again. Tug walked outfielder Willie Wilson. The bases were loaded with just one out.

U. L. Washington came to the plate. The muscular shortstop was chewing his toothpick, as usual. He sacrificed to center. John Wathan raced home from third to make the score 4–1. There were still two men on base. But now there were two outs.

Next, McGraw faced third baseman George Brett. George represented the tying run. He was also the Royals' most dangerous man. He'd had a great season, batting .390. And he'd had a great Series. He'd nailed eight hits so far and scored three runs. He'd done all this in spite of a painful ailment, hemorrhoids.

In fact, any fan in Veterans Stadium would say it had been a great Series all around. The Phillies had taken games 1 and 2. The Royals evened things up by winning games 3 and 4. Then Philadelphia came back with a victory in game 5. Along the way, Larry Bowa drove the Kansas City batters crazy. The Philly shortstop started seven double plays. It was a new Series record. And now . . .

There was a sharp crack. The crowd watched with alarm as Brett laced a hard grounder to deep second. Manny Trillo grabbed the ball. He sent it to first. But the throw pulled Pete Rose off the bag. Brett was safe. The bases were loaded again.

*Shortstop Larry Bowa started seven
double plays for the Phillies in
the 1980 championship battle.
It was a new Series record.*

Hal McRae was the next batter. Hal stayed at the plate for many minutes. Time and again, he fouled off McGraw's pitches. At last, the count was full. Tug let loose with a fast ball. McRae nailed it for a grounder—right to Manny Trillo. This time, Manny's throw to first was on target. The side was out.

The Phillies went down in order in the bottom of the eighth. McGraw came to the mound for the ninth. The fans welcomed him with a great roar. They were telling him that he needed just three more outs. Just three more and the long wait would be over. Philadelphia would have its championship flag.

That great roar grew louder with McGraw's every pitch. Tug slipped a fast ball by outfielder Amos Otis for a called third strike. The noise was now deafening. Otis turned to the plate umpire in a fury. He threw his batting helmet to the dirt. He didn't like the call, and he let the umpire know it. Then he stalked off. He was so angry, he left his batting helmet behind.

The fans were now on their feet. They just couldn't stay seated. Veterans Stadium seemed to be shaking. One away. Just two more to go. . . .

But the Royals were far from dead. Their club had been formed in 1969, and this was their first

Series. They weren't going to go down without a fight. To prove it, first sacker Willie Aikens got on base with a walk. Then John Wathan was back at the plate. He drilled a hard single. So did the man who followed him, Jose Cardenal.

The fans were still on their feet. They were still roaring. But there was fear in their voices. The Royals had loaded the bases in the eighth. And now they'd done it again. Twice in a row. Double trouble!

"Don't lose it now, Tug!" someone yelled.

The next man up was Frank White. He'd fouled out in the eighth. Now he swung hard at a McGraw pitch. But he clipped the ball on its underside. It sailed almost straight up. Then it started to come down on the first base side, in front of the Phillies' dugout. Catcher Bob Boone raced after it. Pete Rose dashed in from first to cover him.

The oddest play in the game was about to occur. Actually, it was the oddest play in the Series.

Boone waved Pete off and moved under the ball. Rose slowed his stride. But still he came on. The ball landed in Boone's mitt—and bounced out!

Rose didn't hesitate a split-second. He threw himself at the ball—and snagged it! Two men were out. The Kansas City runners could not advance.

Later, some of the Royals talked about Rose's catch. One of them said that, right then, he knew the Phillies were going to win. Another one said, "After that catch, I knew there was no way we could win. No way, man."

Rose joked that the whole thing had been a trick play. He said that he and Boone had been practicing it all season.

But there was still one out to go. A grim Willie Wilson came to the plate. Willie ranked as one of the Royals' finest players. He'd posted 280 hits during the season. But he'd slumped in the Series. So far, he'd batted just .154. And he'd struck out 11 times to tie a Series record.

Tug McGraw stood on the mound and looked in for Bob Boone's signs. The roar of the crowd sounded like thunder. McGraw could see a string of Philadelphia police officers. They had come down on the field. They were lined up in front of the stands to hold the happy crowd back if—

"If I don't make any mistakes," McGraw thought.

Pete Rose (above) and Bob Boone (right)
of the Phillies. Together, they made one of
the great catches in the 1980 Series. A high
foul ball hit Bob's mitt and bounced away—
right to the hard-charging Pete.

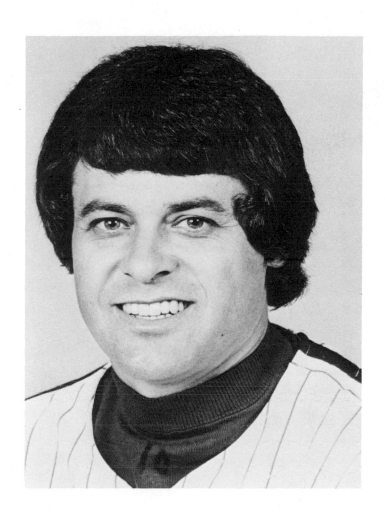

Tug delivered his next pitch. Strike 1! Somehow, the thunder in the stands grew louder. He delivered again. Another strike! There was more thunder. Then Tug pitched again, his best fast ball. He hoped it would be the last one of the game. It was.

Wilson swung hard—at empty air. The ball went past him and thumped into Bob Boone's mitt. Willie threw his bat down in disgust. He had the strikeout record all to himself.

The Series was over. McGraw waved his arms high in triumph. He went dancing off the mound. The Phillies rushed out to crowd around him. They were shouting wildly. But he couldn't hear them above the thunder in the stands. The years of waiting were over. The Phillies had their championship flag.

It's over! Pitcher Tug McGraw's great relief work won the final game of the 1980 Series for the Phillies. And, it gave them the championship. The Series went to six games and Tug relieved in four of them.

1981
LOS ANGELES DODGERS (NL)
vs.
NEW YORK YANKEES (AL)

The next year—1981—was a strange one for baseball. The players went on strike for seven weeks during the season. This caused both leagues to declare two winners in each division—one for the first half of the season, and one for the second half.

As a result, a long series of playoffs had to be held before each league could come up with a pennant winner. Finally, the New York Yankees went against the Los Angeles Dodgers in the World Series. It turned out to be one of the most surprising Series ever played. New York took the first two games and looked sure to win the championship. But then the Dodgers came charging back. They won four games in a row. The baseball crown for 1981 was theirs.

All the games throughout the long history of the Series have been tops. They've given the sports world some of its greatest moments. But there will be more great moments. Because there will always be a World Series—as long as there is a game called baseball and a month called October.

THE WORLD SERIES SINCE 1903

THE WINNERS AND LOSERS

1903
Boston, AL	5
Pittsburgh, NL	3

1904
No Series Held

1905
New York, NL	4
Philadelphia, AL	1

1906
Chicago, AL	4
Chicago, NL	2

1907
Chicago, NL	4
Detroit, AL	0
(1 game tied)	

1908
Chicago, NL	4
Detroit, AL	1

1909
Pittsburgh, NL	4
Detroit, AL	3

1910
Philadelphia, AL	4
Chicago, NL	1

1911
Philadelphia, AL	4
New York, NL	2

1912
Boston, AL	4
New York, NL	3
(1 game tied)	

1913
Philadelphia, AL	4
New York, NL	1

1914
Boston, NL	4
Philadelphia, AL	0

1915
| Boston, AL | 4 |
| Philadelphia, NL | 1 |

1916
| Boston, AL | 4 |
| Brooklyn, NL | 1 |

1917
| Chicago, AL | 4 |
| New York, NL | 2 |

1918
| Boston, AL | 4 |
| Chicago, NL | 2 |

1919 (8 games)
| Cincinnati, NL | 5 |
| Chicago, AL | 3 |

1920
| Cleveland, AL | 5 |
| Brooklyn, NL | 2 |

1921 (8 games)
| New York, NL | 5 |
| New York, AL | 3 |

1922
New York, NL	4
New York, AL	0
(1 game tied)	

1923
| New York, AL | 4 |
| New York, NL | 2 |

1924
| Washington, AL | 4 |
| New York, NL | 3 |

1925
| Pittsburgh, NL | 4 |
| Washington, AL | 3 |

1926
| St. Louis, NL | 4 |
| New York, AL | 3 |

1927
| New York, AL | 4 |
| Pittsburgh, NL | 0 |

1928
| New York, AL | 4 |
| St. Louis, NL | 0 |

1929
| Philadelphia, AL | 4 |
| Chicago, NL | 1 |

1930
| Philadelphia, AL | 4 |
| St. Louis, NL | 2 |

1931
| St. Louis, NL | 4 |
| Philadelphia, AL | 3 |

1932
| New York, AL | 4 |
| Chicago, NL | 0 |

1933
New York, NL   4
Washington, AL   1

1934
St. Louis, NL   4
Detroit, AL   3

1935
Detroit, AL   4
Chicago, NL   2

1936
New York, AL   4
New York, NL   2

1937
New York, AL   4
New York, NL   1

1938
New York, AL   4
Chicago, NL   0

1939
New York, AL   4
Cincinnati, NL   0

1940
Cincinnati, NL   4
Detroit, AL   3

1941
New York, AL   4
Brooklyn, NL   1

1942
St. Louis, NL   4
New York, AL   1

1943
New York, AL   4
St. Louis, NL   1

1944
St. Louis, NL   4
St. Louis, AL   2

1945
Detroit, AL   4
Chicago, NL   3

1946
St. Louis, NL   4
Boston, AL   3

1947
New York, AL   4
Brooklyn, NL   3

1948
Cleveland, AL   4
Boston, NL   2

1949
New York, AL   4
Brooklyn, NL   1

1950
New York, AL   4
Philadelphia, NL   0

1951

| New York, AL | 4 |
| New York, NL | 2 |

1952

| New York, AL | 4 |
| Brooklyn, NL | 3 |

1953

| New York, AL | 4 |
| Brooklyn, NL | 2 |

1954

| New York, NL | 4 |
| Cleveland, AL | 0 |

1955

| Brooklyn, NL | 4 |
| New York, AL | 3 |

1956

| New York, AL | 4 |
| Brooklyn, NL | 3 |

1957

| Milwaukee, NL | 4 |
| New York, AL | 3 |

1958

| New York, AL | 4 |
| Milwaukee, NL | 3 |

1959

| Los Angeles, NL | 4 |
| Chicago, AL | 2 |

1960

| Pittsburgh, NL | 4 |
| New York, AL | 3 |

1961

| New York, AL | 4 |
| Cincinnati, NL | 1 |

1962

| New York, AL | 4 |
| San Francisco, NL | 3 |

1963

| Los Angeles, NL | 4 |
| New York, AL | 0 |

1964

| St. Louis, NL | 4 |
| New York, AL | 3 |

1965

| Los Angeles, NL | 4 |
| Minnesota, AL | 3 |

1966

| Baltimore, AL | 4 |
| Los Angeles, NL | 0 |

1967

| St. Louis, NL | 4 |
| Boston, AL | 3 |

1968

| Detroit, AL | 4 |
| St. Louis, NL | 3 |

1969

New York, NL	4
Baltimore, AL	1

1970

Baltimore, AL	4
Cincinnati, NL	1

1971

Pittsburgh, NL	4
Baltimore, AL	3

1972

Oakland, AL	4
Cincinnati, NL	3

1973

Oakland, AL	4
New York, NL	3

1974

Oakland, AL	4
Los Angeles, NL	1

1975

Cincinnati, NL	4
Boston, AL	3

1976

Cincinnati, NL	4
New York, AL	0

1977

New York, AL	4
Los Angeles, NL	2

1978

New York, AL	4
Los Angeles, NL	2

1979

Pittsburgh, NL	4
Baltimore, AL	3

1980

Philadelphia, NL	4
Kansas City, AL	2

1981

Los Angeles, NL	4
New York, AL	2

INDEX